FROM SEA to SHINING SEA

PENNSYLVANIA

BARBARA A. SOMERVILL

Consultants

MELISSA N. MATUSEVICH, PH.D.

Curriculum and Instruction Specialist
Blacksburg, Virginia

LYNN M. MOSES

School Library Development Advisor
Pennsylvania Department of Education

DONNA L. SCANLON

Manager of Youth Services
Lancaster County Library
Lancaster, Pennsylvania

CHILDREN'S PRESS®
A DIVISION OF SCHOLASTIC INC.

New York • Toronto • London • Auckland • Sydney • Mexico City
New Delhi • Hong Kong • Danbury, Connecticut

Pennsylvania is located in the northeastern United States. It is bordered by New York, New Jersey, Delaware, Maryland, West Virginia, Ohio, and Lake Erie.

The photograph on the front cover shows Gettysburg National Military Park.

Project Editor: Meredith DeSousa
Art Director: Marie O'Neill
Photo Researcher: Marybeth Kavanagh
Design: Robin West, Ox and Company, Inc.
Page 6 map and recipe art: Susan Hunt Yule
All other maps: XNR Productions, Inc.

Library of Congress Cataloging-in-Publication Data

Somervill, Barbara A.
    Pennsylvania / by Barbara A. Somervill.
      v. cm. — (From sea to shining sea)
Includes bibliographical references and index.
Contents: Introducing the Keystone State — The land of Pennsylvania —Pennsylvania
through history — Governing Pennsylvania — The people and places of Pennsylvania —
Pennsylvania almanac — Timeline — Gallery of famous Pennsylvanians.
    ISBN 0-516-22388-7
    1. Pennsylvania—Juvenile literature. [1. Pennsylvania.] I. Title.
    II. Series.
    F149.3 .S66 2002
    974.8—dc21   2002001639

TABLE of CONTENTS

CHAPTER

CHAPTER ONE

INTRODUCING THE KEYSTONE STATE

Philadelphia is not only the state's largest city; it is also the birthplace of our nation.

Pennsylvania is the Liberty Bell and Benjamin Franklin. It is Amish communities and horse-drawn buggies. It is steel mills and coal mines. Pennsylvania is rolling farmland, dense forests, broad rivers, and big cities. It is the birthplace of our nation, and many other things, too.

Pennsylvania is one of the original thirteen colonies. It is called the Keystone State, and rightly so. In a stone or brick arch, the keystone is the center stone. It is the piece that holds the arch together. Look at the original thirteen colonies on a map. Pennsylvania is in the center, holding the northern and southern colonies together. It was the keystone of our early nation.

The state seal depicts Pennsylvania's contributions to our young country. It shows a shield with an American bald eagle on top and olive branches that represent peace along the bottom. On the shield are three symbols: a sailing ship, an old-fashioned plow, and stalks of wheat. Shipping and farming in and around Philadelphia provided the main economy of the Pennsylvania colony. The seal shows the means by which Pennsylvanians earned their money—shipping and farming—when the seal was adopted in 1791.

What comes to mind when you think of Pennsylvania?

- ❖ The Liberty Bell, which cracked beyond repair the first time it was rung
- ❖ Automobile drivers in Lancaster County sharing the road with horse-drawn Amish buggies
- ❖ Hershey, the only town in the world with streetlights in the shape of Hershey's Kisses
- ❖ The state flagship *Niagara*, Oliver Hazard Perry's ship during the War of 1812, docked in Erie
- ❖ The Drake Well Museum in Titusville, which features a reproduction of the first oil well drilled in the United States

Pennsylvania has a long, fascinating story. As you learn more about the state, you'll understand why it was the keystone that held our new nation together in the 1700s. You'll also find out about Pennsylvania's role in both the history and the future of the United States. Turn the page to discover Pennsylvania.

Erie

Pittsburgh

Harrisburg Hershey

Philadelphia

DELAWARE RIVER

©SHY02

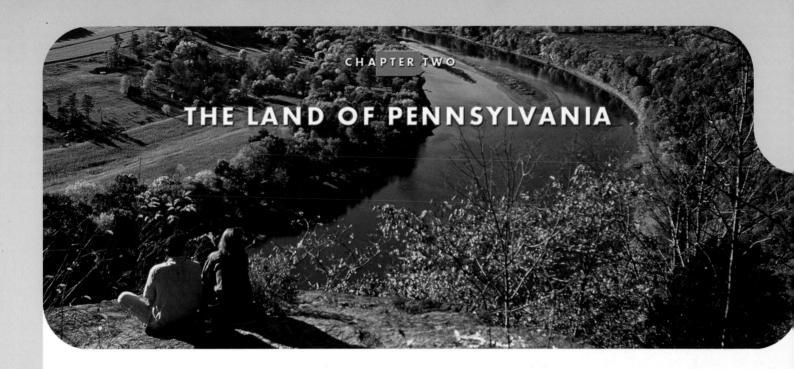

CHAPTER TWO

THE LAND OF PENNSYLVANIA

Pennsylvania is in the northeastern part of the United States. New York and Lake Erie share Pennsylvania's northern border, and New Jersey shares its border to the east. West Virginia and Ohio lie along the western border. Maryland, Delaware, and West Virginia lie to the south.

Pennsylvania is shaped like a rectangle. The eastern boundary (formed by the Delaware River) is irregular, while the other borders are fairly straight. From east to west, Pennsylvania is 307 miles (494 kilometers) long. From north to south, the state measures 169 miles (272 km). Its total area is 46,058 square miles (119,290 square kilometers). There are thirty-two states larger than Pennsylvania.

A couple enjoys a spectacular view of the Susquehanna River Valley.

GEOGRAPHIC REGIONS

Pennsylvania has seven land regions. From east to west, they are the Atlantic Coastal Plain, the New England Upland, the Piedmont, the

Blue Ridge Region, the Appalachian Ridge and Valley, the Allegheny Plateau, and the Erie Lowland.

The Atlantic Coastal Plain

The Atlantic Coastal Plain covers the entire East Coast of the United States, from New York to Florida. It includes a narrow strip of land in the southeast corner of Pennsylvania. The land in this region is low-lying and level, and is cut by the Delaware River and the Schuylkill River.

Some of the nation's best farmland is in the Piedmont.

The New England Upland

The New England Upland is a narrow finger of land jutting into Pennsylvania from New Jersey. The Delaware River separates the region from New Jersey. This area contains low rolling hills and thick forests along the Delaware River. Allentown, Easton, and Bethlehem are main cities in the New England Upland.

The Piedmont

This region spreads out from the Atlantic Coastal Plain to the base of the Appalachian Mountain Range. [The term *piedmont* comes from the French words for foot *(pied)* and mountain *(mont)*.] The piedmont is dotted with farms that produce potatoes, vegetables, and mushrooms. Harrisburg is Pennsylvania's capital city and a major urban center in the Piedmont.

The Blue Ridge Region

The Blue Ridge region extends into the state from Maryland. This small region is hilly and contains excellent farmland. Fruit orchards and dairies dot the land.

The Appalachian Ridge and Valley

The Appalachian Ridge and Valley region covers half the state through the center of Pennsylvania. It is part of the Appalachian Mountains, a mountain range that stretches from Canada to Alabama. Mount Davis, the state's highest point at 3,213 feet (979 m), is found in the southern part of the region near the Maryland border. This area is noted for its rugged mountains, deep valleys, and thick forests. Oats, hay, and livestock are the main agricultural products in the Ridge and Valley region.

Canoeing is a popular activity at the Delaware Water Gap National Recreation Area.

Another popular destination in this area is the Delaware Water Gap. The Delaware Water Gap is a gorge—a long, narrow ravine—that was cut through the Kittatinny Ridge of the Appalachian Mountains by the Delaware River over thousands of years. The Delaware Water Gap National

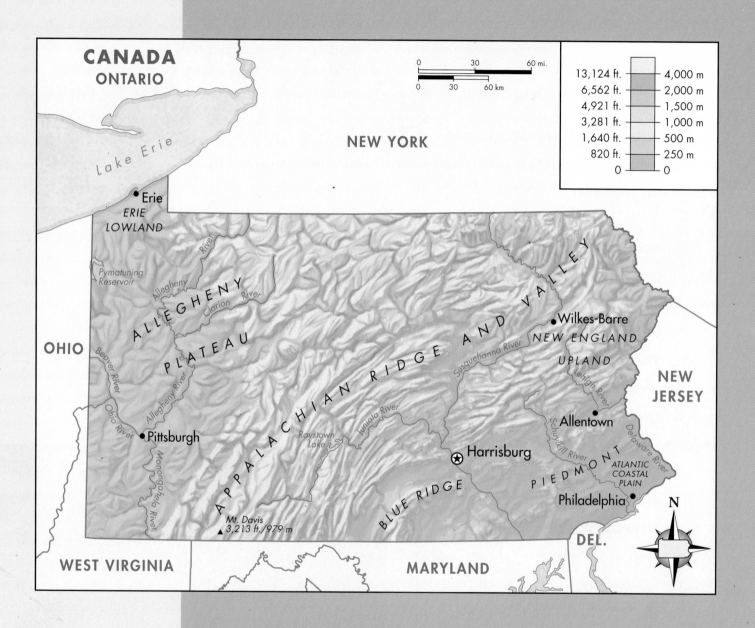

CANADA
ONTARIO

Lake Erie

NEW YORK

13,124 ft. — 4,000 m
6,562 ft. — 2,000 m
4,921 ft. — 1,500 m
3,281 ft. — 1,000 m
1,640 ft. — 500 m
820 ft. — 250 m
0 — 0

30   60 mi.
0   30   60 km

Erie
ERIE
LOWLAND

Pymatuning
Reservoir

ALLEGHENY

PLATEAU

Allegheny River

Clarion River

River

Beaver River

OHIO

Allegheny River

Ohio River

Pittsburgh

Monongahela River

Raystown
Lake

Juniata River

APPALACHIAN RIDGE AND VALLEY

Susquehanna River

Wilkes-Barre

NEW ENGLAND

UPLAND

Lehigh River

Schuylkill River

Allentown

Harrisburg

BLUE RIDGE

Mt. Davis
▲ 3,213 ft./979 m

PIEDMONT

Delaware River

ATLANTIC
COASTAL
PLAIN

Philadelphia

NEW
JERSEY

DEL.

N

WEST VIRGINIA

MARYLAND

Recreation Area serves the Pennsylvania and New Jersey banks of the Delaware River. This 700,000-acre (283,280-hectare) site offers hiking, picnicking, and riverside beaches. The fall is particularly beautiful, when oranges, reds, and golds paint the trees along the riverside.

The Allegheny Plateau

Along the northwest edge of the Appalachian Ridge and Valley is the Allegheny Plateau, sometimes called the Appalachian Plateau. The Allegheny Mountains (part of the Appalachian Mountains) lie within the Appalachian Plateau. Coal and natural gas mines once prospered in this region. The state's second largest city, Pittsburgh, rises up where the Ohio, Monongahela, and Allegheny rivers meet.

In the northern section of the Allegheny Plateau, the Allegheny National Forest provides recreation and natural beauty. The Pocono Mountains are also found in this region. They are a popular place for winter sports and summer vacations.

The Erie Lowland

In the northwest corner of Pennsylvania is the Erie Lowland, the smallest of the seven regions. It lies

Bushkill Falls, located in the Pocono Mountains, is one of Pennsylvania's most famous scenic attractions.

Fishermen try their luck at Presque Isle, a sandy peninsula that juts into Lake Erie.

along the southern part of Lake Erie, one of the Great Lakes. Farms in this area grow grapes and potatoes. Erie is the region's largest city and a major shipping port.

RIVERS AND LAKES

Pennsylvania's land is carved by old, winding rivers. More than 4,500 rivers and streams crisscross the state. The Delaware River forms the state's eastern border. The Susquehanna River cuts through the heart of Pennsylvania. To the west, the Allegheny River twists through low mountains and rolling farmland.

Rivers flowing eastward include the Delaware and the Susquehanna, which feed into Maryland's Chesapeake Bay. In the west, the Allegheny and Monongahela rivers join together at Pittsburgh to form the Ohio River, eventually emptying into the Mississippi River. Smaller rivers, creeks, and streams throughout the state flow into these large rivers. These tributaries include the Juniata, Schuylkill, Lehigh, Beaver, and Clarion rivers.

Few of the more than 300 lakes in Pennsylvania are natural lakes; most are manmade. Manmade lakes are formed by people building dams across rivers and flooding the valleys. The largest is Raystown Lake in south central Pennsylvania, about 12 square miles (31 sq km).

This lake was formed by a dam on the Juniata River. Visitors can enjoy fishing and boating on the lake, as well as hiking and camping at Rothrock State Forest, the area surrounding Raystown Lake.

The state also has 40 miles (64 km) of lakeshore along Lake Erie. Lake Erie provides major shipping opportunities. Ships move through the lakes, along the St. Lawrence River, and into the Atlantic Ocean.

PLANTS AND ANIMALS

Pennsylvania is heavily forested. More than half the state is forestland, where dark green pines stand side by side with leafy elms and oaks. Some 2 million acres (809,356 hectares) of forestland are part of Pennsylvania's state forest system. The state's Bureau of Forestry protects sixty-one natural areas and fourteen wilderness areas, although lumbering is allowed in many forest areas.

The Appalachian Mountains burst with color in autumn.

The most common trees are elm, maple, beech, birch, sycamore, oak, pine, and hemlock. Within the forests, berries and shrubs are everywhere. Blackberry thickets, wild cherry, and blueberries dot the woodland. Wild ginger, wild mint, azaleas, dogwoods, and rhododendron sprinkle color throughout the springtime forests and meadows.

Many large mammals were hunted to extinction during colonial days. However, there are still some black bears living in the northwestern forest areas. The rugged forests also provide homes for white-tailed deer, raccoons, beaver, rabbits, small rodents, insects, birds, and skunks.

EXTRA! EXTRA!

The eastern puma or cougar (felis concolor cougar) is one of Pennsylvania's endangered species. Many of these sleek, tawny-colored cats once roamed from eastern Canada south to Tennessee. Today, there are few eastern pumas left in the wild because hunters trapped and killed the species. The U.S. Fish and Wildlife Service recently completed a program to reintroduce the eastern puma in wilderness areas of the Appalachian Range. If the programs are successful, eastern pumas may also be placed in remote areas of the Appalachian Ridge and Valley.

CLIMATE

Pennsylvania has a moderate climate. Summers are hot and wet, with thunder and lightning storms often crashing through the skies. July days in Philadelphia have an average high temperature of 86° Fahrenheit (22° Celsius). Pennsylvania's mountain areas tend to be cooler than Philadelphia, which is closer to the Atlantic coast. The average summer temperature in Philadelphia is about 8 degrees warmer than the average summer temperature in Altoona in the Appalachians. The hottest Pennsylvania temperature on record was 111° F (44° C) on July 10, 1936, at Phoenixville.

Winters in Pennsylvania are cold and snowy. The average January temperature across the state is only 28° F (–2° C). The coldest temperature ever recorded was a brisk –42° F (–41° C) on January 5, 1904, at Smethport.

Pennsylvania weather is not easy to predict. Winds off Lake Erie can bring sudden summer storms or winter snows. Dry weather from the southwest brings warm winds and pleasant sunny days. Weather patterns change quickly, and visitors are always warned to bring a sweater, sunscreen, and an umbrella. The state averages 42 inches (107 cm) of precipitation yearly, in the form of rain, sleet, hail, and snow. Pittsburgh, in the west, experiences about 117 days of precipitation yearly, while Philadelphia, in the east, has an average of 154 days of precipitation.

The snow blankets this covered bridge in Lancaster County.

CHAPTER THREE

PENNSYLVANIA THROUGH HISTORY

Philadelphians hear a reading of the Declaration of Independence from the steps of Independence Hall in 1776.

People have lived in what we now call Pennsylvania since about 10,000 B.C. These early people were hunter-gatherers. They hunted large mammals, such as mammoths, bison, and bears, as their main food supply. They also gathered nuts, berries, fruits, and roots for food. These people did not set up villages because they needed to travel to find game animals. Today, we know very little about them. The only clues that show how they lived are stone tools and bits of pottery discovered along the Susquehanna and Monongahela rivers.

Over hundreds of years, the early people went from being hunter-gatherers to being farmers. They cleared land and planted crops, including corn, beans, and squash. They built permanent houses and set up towns. Most of these early towns were built near rivers or streams.

By A.D. 1500, there were many established Native American tribes living in today's Pennsylvania. These tribes included the Lenape, the

Susquehannock, and several small tribes in the western part of the state.

The Lenape lived in the east, mainly along what are now called the Delaware and Brandywine rivers. Many Lenape also lived along the Lehigh River. They called themselves "original people." The Lenape spoke a style of Algonquian, a language spoken by many tribes in northeastern North America. They were hunters and farmers. Men hunted deer, bears, and rabbits, or fished for trout, carp, and catfish. They also collected crabs and oysters. Lenape women farmed the land. They planted corn, beans, pumpkins, and squash. They also collected wild herbs that were used for medicines and to season food.

The Susquehannock lived in the central part of today's Pennsylvania. They were also hunters and farmers. The Susquehannock spoke Iroquoian, the language of the Iroquois Confederacy. The Iroquois Confederacy was a powerful group of Native American tribes that lived mostly in present-day New York, including the Mohawk, Iroquois, Onondaga, Oneida, Cayuga, Seneca, and Tuscarora. Although the Susquehannock were not part of the Iroquois Confederacy, they were neighbors and traded with the Iroquois.

Early Native Americans in Pennsylvania harvested maize, or corn.

Like their Iroquois neighbors, the Susquehannock lived in long-houses. These houses had many rooms inside and usually housed several families at one time. By living together, adults shared chores such as hunting, childcare, cooking, and sewing. The Susquehanna River is named for the Susquehannock, who lived along the river's banks.

The Monongahela, Shawnee, Huron, and Erie tribes lived in the west. They hunted with bows and arrows, as did the Lenape and the Susquehannock. Game animals included bears, deer, wild turkeys, geese, ducks, squirrels, and rabbits. Roots, berries, and farm crops were also part of their food supply.

THE DECLINE OF NATIVE AMERICANS

In the early 1600s, Dutch sailors from Holland began exploring the areas we call New York, New Jersey, and eastern Pennsylvania. The Dutch traded guns with the Iroquois in exchange for furs and animal skins, which were used to make hats, collars, and other clothing. With these guns, the Iroquois went to war against the Huron and the Erie and almost wiped out both tribes. The Iroquois also attacked the Susquehannock, who were defeated by the Iroquois and driven from their lands.

Guns were not the only killers of the native people. European diseases, such as

Native Americans traded furs with the Dutch settlers in exchange for European goods.

smallpox, chicken pox, and measles, infected and killed entire tribes because the native people had no resistance to these diseases. Disease may have been responsible for the end of the Monongahela tribe, who completely disappeared around 1650. Before the arrival of Europeans, there were about 20,000 Native Americans in the area. War, disease, and forced removal from tribal lands reduced the native population to only 1,000 by 1790, when the first United States census was taken.

THE EUROPEANS ARRIVE

The first European known to explore the land we call Pennsylvania was Cornelius Mey, a Dutch explorer. Mey traveled up the Delaware River in 1614 and explored the area near present-day Chester. However, Mey did not set up a colony.

Swedish settlers built the first permanent European settlement in Pennsylvania in 1643. Their colony, called New Sweden, was located just south of today's Philadelphia and spread eastward to Wilmington, Delaware. The Swedes built Fort Christina for protection from Native Americans. Both within the fort's walls and nearby, the Swedes built homes made of logs. Log cabins were not held together by nails, but by cutting notches in each log and fitting the logs together. Eventually, log cabins became the standard style of house for people living on the frontier.

Swedish settlers soon came in conflict with the Dutch, who had explored along the Delaware River. The Swedes and the Dutch argued over fur trading rights and land. In 1654, the Swedes took over a Dutch

Early settlers of New Sweden built small settlements along the Delaware River.

trading post by force. The next year, Peter Stuyvesant, the governor of Dutch New Netherland, attacked the Swedes and seized the Swedish settlements for the Dutch.

However, neither the Swedes nor the Dutch kept their Pennsylvania property for long. In 1664, England seized New Netherland from the Dutch. The English also took over today's Pennsylvania, which had been under Dutch control for ten years.

PENN'S CHARTER

In 1681, an Englishman named William Penn received a royal charter from King Charles II. A royal charter is a document given by a king or queen to a person or group. The charter Penn received gave him the right to found a colony on land taken from the Dutch. (European kings from Spain, France, and England believed that if an explorer representing their country claimed land, it automatically belonged to that explorer's king. The fact that native people lived on the land did not matter to the kings, who saw no problem giving the land away as a gift.)

Penn sailed to his land in 1682 aboard the ship *Welcome*. With Penn were families of Quakers, a religious group that believed in peace and

friendship. Penn's new colony was called Pennsylvania, meaning "Penn's Woods," after Penn's father. Penn set up the first permanent English settlement in Pennsylvania and called it Philadelphia, the city of brotherly love. His plan was to welcome people of all religions, and to set up a government run by the people. He felt this way because Quakers and other religious groups were often tormented in Europe. The name given to Penn's plan was the "Holy Experiment." Penn placed ads in European newspapers, encouraging people to come to Pennsylvania.

William Penn laid out the streets of Philadelphia in 1682.

THE WALKING PURCHASE

During William Penn's life, relations between the settlers and the Lenape remained friendly. However, Penn's followers did not treat the Lenape as fairly as Penn had. In 1737, the settlers made an agreement with the Lenape to buy land. The Lenape agreed to sell the colonists as much land as a man could walk in a day and a half. The Lenape expected the "walk" to be made by one man walking, resting, and eating. However, the colonists had several men run relays to mark the land being purchased. In this way, they cheated the Lenape out of a large parcel of land.

COLONIAL DAYS

During the early 1700s, Pennsylvania thrived. Its main city, Philadelphia, increased in both population and importance. The city had a fire department, a newspaper, and a modern hospital. Philadelphia's lending library, a program started by Benjamin Franklin, was the first library of this type in the colonies. Rows of houses sprang up, and roads were built.

The city quickly became a center of industry and shipping because of its easy access to the Atlantic Ocean and its natural harbor on the Delaware River. Merchants bought finished goods from England and France, and shipped raw materials, such as lumber and fur pelts, to Europe for sale. From as early as 1750, Pennsylvania's iron mills forged metal goods for the colonies and for shipment to England.

EXTRA! EXTRA!

Colonial leaders often disagreed about the borders of their land. Two such leaders, the Calverts of Maryland and the Penns of Pennsylvania, argued over the boundary between their lands. They hired Charles Mason and Jeremiah Dixon to establish a border. Using surveying methods, the pair determined the exact borderline and marked it with large stones. This task, begun in 1763, took four years to complete. The boundary line between Pennsylvania and Maryland is known as the Mason-Dixon line. It served as the dividing line between North and South during the Civil War.

In western Pennsylvania, the London-based Ohio Company built a trading post in 1749, named Fort Prince George. The Ohio Company claimed land from Virginia north through the Ohio River Valley. The French, who had already claimed the Ohio River Valley, saw this as a threat. Both the French and the English wanted furs and land in the area.

During the 1750s, the French built a string of forts from Lake Erie to the Ohio River. One of these forts was Fort Duquesne, on the site of today's Pittsburgh. The French wished to protect their fur trading interests from the English.

In 1754, young George Washington led 150 Virginia militia to see how many French soldiers were at Fort Duquesne. The Virginians came

FAMOUS FIRSTS

- The first U.S. mint for printing and coining money was in Philadelphia.
- Benjamin Franklin opened the first lending library in 1731 in Philadelphia.
- The first symphony orchestra in the colonies played for the first time in 1744 in Pennsylvania.
- The first antislavery organization in the United States formed in Philadelphia in 1775.
- In 1780, Pennsylvania became the first state to abolish slavery.
- The Philadelphia Zoo was the first zoo in America.
- The first commercial radio station, KDKA, began broadcasting from Pittsburgh in 1920.

British soldiers marched on Fort Duquesne during the French and Indian War.

upon a small troop of French soldiers and ambushed them. The French were so angered by this act that they chased after Washington's men, who quickly built Fort Necessity at Great Meadows for protection.

This attack began the French and Indian War (1754–1763). British and colonial forces fought the French and many Native American tribes throughout the northeast. Many Native Americans sided with the French because the French accepted the native way of life. The British continually tried to force a "civilized" lifestyle on native people, which they resented.

Eventually, the British forced the French from Fort Duquesne and renamed the site Fort Pitt, which grew into the city of Pittsburgh. When the war ended after seven years, the French lost their claim on all land east of the Mississippi River, except for New Orleans.

THE MAKING OF A REVOLUTION

Once the fighting ended, Great Britain (England) needed to find a way to pay the costs of the war. To raise money, the British government passed a number of tax laws against the colonies. These included the Stamp Act, the Townshend Act, and the Quartering Act. These laws required the colonists to pay taxes (extra money) for goods such as tea, sugar, glass, printed materials, and a long list of other common household items.

Angered by these taxes, the people rebelled. The colonists wanted a government that listened to its problems. The British government was too far away to understand the burdens of colonial life. In an effort to be heard, the thirteen colonies held a meeting called the First Continental Congress.

In 1774, each of the thirteen colonies sent representatives to the First Continental Congress, held in Philadelphia's Carpenters' Hall. Philadelphia became the center of the movement for freedom from Great Britain. At the first Continental Congress, the members passed a statement of personal rights and made a list of reasons why they disagreed with Great Britain's tax programs. King George III ignored their feelings.

On July 4, 1776, members of the Second Continental Congress adopted the Declaration of Independence. This document announced the colonies' freedom from Great Britain. According to the declaration, the colonies would be independent, but they were united in the fight for freedom. Representatives Benjamin Franklin, Robert Morris, John

Members of the Continental Congress discuss the Declaration of Independence.

Morton, George Ross, Benjamin Rush, James Smith, George Taylor, and James Wilson signed the document on behalf of Pennsylvania. The Continental Congress also formed an army under General George Washington. These two events led to the start of the Revolutionary War (1775–1783), in which the colonies fought against Great Britain for freedom.

Pennsylvania was the site of several important battles during the American Revolution. In 1777, the British defeated the colonists at the Battle of Brandywine, and again at Germantown. Washington's army, short on food, clothing, ammunition, and medicine, spent the winter at Valley Forge. The hardships suffered by the colonial troops were recorded in the journal of Dr. Albigence Waldo, a surgeon at Valley Forge: "I am sorely out of humour. Poor food—hard lodging—cold weather—fatigue—nasty clothing. . . I can't endure it."

The colonists eventually won the Revolutionary War. At the Constitutional Convention in 1787, representatives from each new state wrote a list of rules—a constitution—that established the new government. Each state would have its own leaders and lawmakers, while the United States government, called the federal government, would lead the Union.

Under the United States Constitution, the country's leader would be a president elected by the people. George Washington became the first United States president. On December 12, 1787, Pennsylvania became the second of the original thirteen states. Philadelphia served as the capital of the new country from 1790 to 1800, when the federal government moved to Washington, D.C.

WHO'S WHO IN PENNSYLVANIA?

Mrs. Mary Hays ("Molly Pitcher" c. 1754–1832) gained fame for helping the Continental army during the Revolutionary War. At the Battle of Monmouth in New Jersey, Hays carried pitchers of water to thirsty soldiers on the battlefield. Called Molly Pitcher by the troops, she came to represent all women who helped the troops during the war. Hays lived in Carlisle.

WHO'S WHO IN PENNSYLVANIA?

Betsy Ross (1752–1836) was a seamstress (someone who makes a living by sewing) in Philadelphia. Many people believe that Ross made the first American flag. According to legend, George Washington visited Ross in June 1776 and asked her to make a flag according to a sketch he provided. As the story goes, Washington wanted six-pointed stars, but Mrs. Ross insisted on five-pointed stars. Whether any of this story is true cannot be proven. However, Betsy Ross did make flags for the Pennsylvania Navy, and her home is a popular tourist site in Philadelphia.

WHAT'S IN A NAME?

The names of many places in Pennsylvania have interesting origins.

Name	Comes From or Means
Bellefonte	French for "beautiful fountain"
Forty Fort	Named for the first forty settlers in Pennsylvania
Susquehanna River	Named for the Susquehannock people
Bird-in-Hand	A tavern sign with a picture of a bird on a hand
Philadelphia	Greek for "brotherly love"
Delaware River	Named for England's Lord de La Warr
Wilkes-Barre	Named for John Wilkes and Isaac Barre, founding fathers

It wasn't long before the United States and Great Britain were at war again. This time, it was on the seas. In the early 1800s, British sailors captured U.S. ships and forced the sailors to work on British ships. This act, called impressment, eventually led to the War of 1812.

The War of 1812 (1812–1815) was fought in the Atlantic Ocean and also on the Great Lakes. Because the young United States had no navy on the Great Lakes, Pennsylvania's carpenters, shipbuilders, and sailors hurried to build a fleet of ships. Captain Oliver Hazard Perry led this fleet, built in only a matter of weeks.

On September 10, 1813, the tiny U.S. fleet faced the larger, more experienced British fleet in the Battle of Lake Erie. Surprisingly, Perry's fleet won the battle. After the victory, Perry sent this message: "We have met the enemy and they are ours." This battle, a turning point in the war, showed that the United States could challenge the more powerful British—and win a battle.

The Battle of Lake Erie gave control of the Great Lakes area to the United States.

CONNECTING EAST AND WEST

In the early 1800s, canals (man-made waterways) were built to connect the state's major rivers. A series of canals, called the Pennsylvania Main Line Canal system, stretched 300 miles (484 km) across the state. To cross the mountains in central Pennsylvania, a series of inclined planes were built. Heavy barges were pulled over mountain areas along the inclined planes.

Although the canal system was a success, it was not as quick or efficient as the railroad. By 1829, one in every four miles of railroad track in the United States ran through Pennsylvania. Railroads connected mines, farms, and mills to markets across the nation.

Philadelphia and Pittsburgh served as the state's shipping hubs. About 900 ships could dock in Philadelphia at any time. These ships transported goods to and from Europe and other East Coast ports, such as Boston and Charleston. In the west, Pittsburgh's location provided shipping along the Ohio River to the Mississippi. Steel, iron, coal, and farm products were shipped by barge or steamship along the Ohio River.

THE INDUSTRIAL AGE

Pennsylvania had a strong background in iron work, as well as abundant forestlands for lumbering and shipping along the Delaware River. The combination of skilled workers and rich natural resources made Pennsylvania ideal for industrial development. As steel replaced iron in the mid-1800s, the state became the heart of the country's steel industry. Pittsburgh, in particular, became a leading steel-producing city.

Where there were steel mills, fuel was needed. Pennsylvania's coal mines provided fuel to support iron and steel mills. As railroads and steamboats became popular, Pennsylvania coal also fueled the large steam engines that ran trains and ships.

Coal was not Pennsylvania's only resource. In the 1840s, Samuel Kier of Pittsburgh experimented with oil he found seeping out of the ground. He distilled the dark, thick oil, which he then used for lamp fuel. Up to this point in time, there were no electric lights, only oil lamps, which burned expensive whale oil. Kier's new lamp oil, called kerosene, was more affordable to produce. His discovery led to a new resource-based industry for Pennsylvania—oil refining. Refineries to process the raw oil sprang up throughout western Pennsylvania; refined oil was then sent by railroad to major cities. This made kerosene available to everyone.

In 1859, Edwin Drake drilled the world's first oil well near Titusville. Drake hit oil at 70 feet (21 m). In the 1860s, people drilled oil wells all across western Pennsylvania, much as gold miners dug for gold in California during the Gold Rush.

A crowd gathers to watch a gushing oil well near Titusville.

ANTISLAVERY AND THE CIVIL WAR

While iron giants sped along Pennsylvania's railroad tracks, another type of "railroad" was in action—the Underground Railroad. As early as 1688, Pennsylvania's German population spoke out against slavery, the practice of "owning" Africans and forcing them to work for a master, usually a white landowner. Slavery supported the cotton-based economy in the South, where wealthy plantation owners kept slaves to plow, seed, and harvest their land. In 1780, Pennsylvania became the first state to forbid slavery.

Because many Pennsylvanians, including the Quakers and the Amish, were against slavery, they often helped slaves to escape. The escape route was part of the Underground Railroad, which operated in several Northern states, including Pennsylvania. This was not a railroad,

Many Quakers helped runaway slaves escape capture by secretly guiding them from one safe house to the next.

nor was it underground. It was a series of safe homes, hiding places, and people that enabled slaves to make a safe journey to Canada, where they could be free. The term *underground* described the hidden, secret nature of the system. About 100,000 slaves escaped along the Underground Railroad.

In 1860, Abraham Lincoln was elected president of the United States. Southern states knew of Lincoln's antislavery views. They expected the United States government to pass laws ending slavery. Because cotton production, the main industry of the South, depended heavily on slave labor, an end to slavery would hurt their economy. Southern states also believed that each state should be able to make their own decision about slavery, and that the United States government should not be more powerful than each separate state.

Even before Lincoln was sworn in as president, Southern states began to secede, or leave the Union, over slavery and states' rights. The Southern states formed a new nation called the Confederate States of America.

In April 1861, Confederate forces fired on Fort Sumter in Charleston, South Carolina. This action was the first battle of the Civil War

(1861–1865). Twenty-five regiments of young Pennsylvanian men signed up to fight for the Union (the North), and headed off to war. The battles were fierce. Lists of dead and wounded arrived in Pennsylvania's cities and towns, and many people wondered if the war was worth fighting.

In 1863, the only battle held on Pennsylvania soil took place. This was the Battle of Gettysburg, and it cost more lives than any other battle fought in North America. General George Meade led the Union army, while General George E. Pickett commanded the Confederate troops. In this battle, which was a turning point of the war, the Union lost more than 23,000 men; the South lost over 20,000. Confederate Captain Joseph Graham summed up the battle in a letter: ". . . our supplies were exhausted. . . And for want of transportation, we left about 4,500 wounded to fall into their [Union] hands. Neither side buried the dead of July 3rd before leaving. It was an awful affair altogether." In 1863, a few months after the battle, President Lincoln gave his famous Gettysburg Address, when the battleground was named a national cemetery.

In 1865, Confederate General Robert E. Lee surrendered to Union General Ulysses S. Grant at Appomattox Courthouse in Virginia. In all, about 380,000 Pennsylvanians served during the Civil War.

President Lincoln gave a short—but memorable—speech at the battlefield in Gettysburg.

Carnegie Steel workers operate a Bessemer Converter, a huge machine that changed pig iron into steel.

Once the war was over, Pennsylvanians returned to building their industrial empire. Along with the rise of industry came the rise of industrial leaders. The best-known Pennsylvania industrial leader was Andrew Carnegie. It was Carnegie who brought steel manufacturing to Pennsylvania.

Andrew Carnegie set up steel mills at Braddock and Homestead in the 1870s. They were located near Pittsburgh because the milling process required coke—a coal-based product—and Pittsburgh was a center for coal mining and coke production. Henry Frick controlled most of Pittsburgh's coal and coke. Carnegie and Frick formed the Carnegie Steel Company. The partnership grew quickly, and both men became rich. Less than thirty years later, Carnegie Steel joined with other steel mills to form the U.S. Steel Corporation. The new corporation owned 149 steel mills, coal mines, railroads, and ships. By the early 1900s, U.S. Steel and Bethlehem Steel led Pennsylvania's steel industry. These giants produced most of the steel in the United States.

WHO'S WHO IN PENNSYLVANIA?

Andrew Carnegie (1835–1919) was not just an industrial giant. He also gave more than $350 million to charities. Among his favorite charitable acts was building 2,500 libraries across the United States. Carnegie once said, "He who dies rich, dies disgraced." Carnegie lived in Pittsburgh.

While coal mines and steel mills made the owners rich, those who worked in the mines and mills faced poverty. They suffered long hours, poor working conditions, and low pay. In some mines, six- and seven-year-old boys picked coal out of waste rock. At the age of twelve, they worked down in the mines. Miners regularly faced mine fires, tunnel collapses, and serious injuries. Those who survived the working conditions often came down with black lung disease, a deadly condition that came from breathing coal dust.

Mining and loading coal was a dangerous and difficult job.

In an effort to improve their situation, some miners formed a secret organization called the Molly Maguires. Members of this group attacked managers from the mining companies. They threatened police and judges. The Molly Maguires used terror tactics to reach their goals.

Not all efforts ended in violence, however. During the late 1800s, many workers joined the National Progressive Union of Miners and Mine Laborers (later called the United Mine Workers of America). Labor unions organized groups of workers so they could fight for better working conditions and wages. The union's goals included fewer hours, shorter workweeks, better pay, health benefits, and safer working conditions. Workers hoped to discuss these problems with mine owners and reach solutions.

When they could not get these improvements, the miners went on strike, or stopped work, in 1875. After five months, the strike had accomplished very little. Strikebreakers (people to take the place of striking union members) poured into Pennsylvania's mining towns. Strikers ran out of money because they were not working. Many lost their homes, and their families went hungry. Eventually, however, the unions succeeded in getting better working conditions and pay for their members, without using the violence of the Molly Maguires.

THE TWENTIETH CENTURY

When World War I (1914–1918) broke out in Europe, the United States chose to stay out of the war. By 1917, however, this became impossible. German ships had begun to attack and sink American civilian ships. The United States joined sides with Great Britain, France, and other countries against Germany and Austria-Hungary.

Pennsylvania steel became a valuable product during the war. It was used for everything from guns and ammunition to helmets. Shipyards used Pennsylvania steel for building destroyers, cruisers, and other types of ships. When the war was over, steel continued to be in high demand for automobiles, eating utensils, and other things.

In 1929, America's long period of prosperity came to a quick end. A serious economic setback sent the country into a financial panic. This difficult time, called the Great Depression (1929–1939), hit Pennsylvania hard.

In the beginning, there were more products produced than there were people to buy them. Money lost much of its value. In New York, the stock market fell because investments (shares) in businesses and banks had become worthless. Banks could not pay out money from savings and checking accounts because there wasn't enough money to go around. Instead, banks locked their doors and went out of business. People with money in those banks lost everything.

In Pennsylvania, four thousand coal mines closed. More than half of all steelworkers lost their jobs. Across the state, only farmworkers continued to have regular work and income. During the depression, eight in ten workers in Pittsburgh were jobless.

To overcome the effects of the Great Depression, the state government passed the Talbot Act. This law created new jobs building public roads and buildings. Under the Talbot Act, the state built the Pennsylvania Turnpike, a highway across the state. However, the Talbot Act and efforts by the federal government could not stop the depression. Only a war could do that.

WORLD WAR II

European countries also struggled during the Great Depression. In an effort to gain land and seaports, Germany invaded the neighboring country of Poland on September 1, 1939. Within days, Great Britain and France declared war on Germany. Within months, almost all of Europe had joined either the Allies (England, France, and Russia) or the Axis powers (Germany, Austria, and Italy) in World War II (1939–1945). The United States chose to stay out of the war. However, the war in Europe put Americans back to work.

The African-American 369th Infantry marched in a World War II parade in Pittsburgh in 1942.

Companies in the United States began to sell war materials to the Allies. Suddenly, factories that had closed during the depression reopened, clamoring for workers. Pennsylvania produced the second largest amount of war goods, and provided coal and steel during the war. Pennsylvania shipyards produced one in every four ships launched by the U.S. Navy. Pennsylvania steel formed the armor on tanks, the bodies of jeeps, and the structures of planes.

In 1941, the Japanese attacked Pearl Harbor, a United States naval base in Hawaii, and the United States entered World War II. More than one million Pennsylvanians served in the military during the war. The prosperity that began at the start of the war lasted throughout the 1950s and into the early 1960s.

By the 1960s, Pennsylvania's industries were in trouble. The steel industry struggled as factories began buying cheaper steel from Japan and other Asian countries. By 1970, roughly one-third of the state's steelworkers was jobless. Oil-burning or natural gas furnaces replaced coal for heating. Electrical and transportation equipment, once major Pennsylvania industries, also lost out to foreign companies. Job loss and business closings continue to affect Pennsylvanians.

PENNSYLVANIA TODAY

Environmental issues concern many Pennsylvanians today. In 1957, the country's first nuclear power plant was completed at Three Mile Island on the Susquehanna River. The plant was expected to produce safe, inexpensive electrical power. However, on March 28, 1979, radioactive steam escaped from the plant, creating the worst nuclear accident in our country's history. (Radioactive steam is water vapor that includes harmful energy rays. These rays can cause sickness or death.) Because of this accident, many people protested the use of nuclear energy. Others feel that this "near disaster" caused the nuclear power industry to develop better protection against future accidents.

The crisis at Three Mile Island drew national attention and concern over the safety of nuclear energy. The undamaged reactor is still in operation today.

FIND OUT MORE

The accident at Three Mile Island released harmful radiation. Radiation—radioactive energy rays—can cause serious health problems. However, it can also be used to help sick people. Find out how radiation is used to make sick people healthy.

Mine fires and chemical waste products are other environmental problems. For almost forty years, coal mines near Centralia have smoldered beneath the ground. In some areas, smoke escapes through cracks in the ground. No firefighting techniques can stop the burning. In addition, factory waste products dumped into the state's rivers caused serious pollution. In 1988, a major oil spill on the Monongahela and Ohio Rivers added still more problems.

To address environmental issues, Pennsylvania developed the Clean Air Act Amendments of 1990, which helped to reduce factory air pollution. The Pennsylvania Land Recycling Program of 1995 cleans polluted soil and finds new uses for cleaned land. Both programs improve the quality of Pennsylvania's environment.

The end of Pennsylvania's steel giants brought economic problems to the state. Competition from foreign countries caused many steel mills to close. This led to other problems, such as empty buildings, homeless people, and poor housing. The state encouraged new industries to move to Pennsylvania, including computer companies and electronics industries. In addition, tourism has become a major source of income for Pennsylvania.

Both Pittsburgh and Philadelphia have begun major urban renewal projects. City blocks have been rebuilt, new business brought in, and housing improved. Pittsburgh's program has been so successful that the city was named the best major American city to live in during the 1980s. Philadelphia, a city in which four in ten people are African-

American, elected its first African-American mayor, Wilson Goode, in 1984. State programs, urban renewal, and new industry will continue to improve the quality of life for Pennsylvanians.

CHAPTER FOUR

GOVERNING PENNSYLVANIA

Pennsylvania is a commonwealth. Citizens choose their leaders by vote, as in other states. In a commonwealth, important officials such as judges and department heads are also elected; in other states these officials are often appointed by the governor. The idea behind a commonwealth goes back to colonial days, before the United States was formed.

The gold dome of the capitol building gleams high above the city of Harrisburg.

THE STATE CONSTITUTION

When William Penn founded the Pennsylvania colony, he set up a government that was run for and by its people. Penn's idea was for the people to have representatives who would speak for their town or region, and advise Penn about laws. Penn also said that the government would not be controlled by any religion. All these ideas were set down in a document called Penn's Charter.

FIND OUT MORE

Pennsylvania is one of four states that are called commonwealths. What other states are commonwealths?

Today, Penn's Charter is kept in Harrisburg. Some people think of it as the state's "birth certificate." When the colonies declared their independence and set up state governments, Pennsylvania based its state constitution on the ideas in Penn's Charter.

Pennsylvania's first constitution was written in 1776, the same year the Declaration of Independence was signed. Since then, Pennsylvania has had new constitutions in 1790, 1838, 1874, 1968, and 1999. The constitution can also be amended, or changed. Lawmakers suggest changes, which are voted on by the legislature (Pennsylvania's lawmaking body). If they vote in favor of the change, the amendment then goes to the people for approval.

The constitution contains the plan for running the state government. Specific jobs are divided among three groups, called branches: the executive, the legislative, and the judicial. All branches have equal power, which helps to keep the government running smoothly.

EXECUTIVE BRANCH

The executive branch makes sure laws are enforced. The governor is the chief executive or leader of Pennsylvania. He or she is responsible for running the state. The governor also represents Pennsylvania in dealing with other states, as well as the United States government.

The governor is in charge of overseeing several state departments. These include education, transportation, law enforcement, taxation, environmental protection, and agriculture, among other things.

The governor appoints people to run each of these departments.

Pennsylvanians elect a governor for a four-year term, and governors cannot serve more than two terms in a row. Supporting the governor are other elected officials, including the lieutenant governor, the attorney general, the state treasurer, and the state auditor. These officials may also serve multiple terms, but never more than two terms in a row.

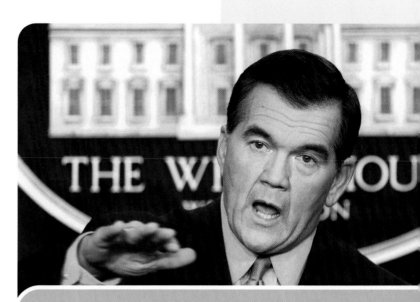

WHO'S WHO IN PENNSYLVANIA?

Tom Ridge (1945–) was governor of Pennsylvania from 1995 to 2001, when President George W. Bush appointed him the first director of the Office of Homeland Security in the history of the United States. As director, he is in charge of protecting Americans against terrorist threats and attacks from other countries. He was born in Pittsburgh.

LEGISLATIVE BRANCH

The legislature makes state laws. Called the General Assembly, it is made up of two parts: a senate and a house of representatives. There are 50 senators, and each serves a four-year term. There are 203 representatives; each serves a two-year term.

Bills, or proposed new laws, can be suggested in either the senate or the house of representatives. Ideas for new laws may come from lawmakers, businesses, professional groups such as the Pennsylvania Bar Association (lawyers), or from average citizens. A committee reviews each bill to see if it meets the needs of the people. Once the bill is approved by the committee, it is brought up for a vote. For a bill to

PENNSYLVANIA GOVERNORS

Name	Term	Name	Term
Thomas Mifflin	1790–1799	Samuel Whitaker Pennypacker	1903–1907
Thomas McKean	1799–1808	Edwin Sydney Stuart	1907–1911
Simon Snyder	1808–1817	John Kinley Tener	1911–1915
William Findlay	1817–1820	Martin Grove Brumbaugh	1915–1919
Joseph Hiester	1820–1823	William Cameron Sproul	1919–1923
John Andrew Schulze	1823–1829	Gifford Pinchot	1923–1927
George Wolf	1829–1835	John Stuchell Fisher	1927–1931
Joseph Ritner	1835–1839	Gifford Pinchot	1931–1935
David Rittenhouse Porter	1839–1845	George Howard Earle	1935–1939
Francis Rawn Shunk	1845–1848	Arthur Horace James	1939–1943
William Freame Johnston	1848–1852	Edward Martin	1943–1947
William Bigler	1852–1855	John C. Bell, Jr.	1947
James Pollock	1855–1858	James H. Duff	1947–1951
William Fisher Packer	1858–1861	John S. Fine	1951–1955
Andrew Gregg Curtin	1861–1867	George Michael Leader	1955–1959
John White Geary	1867–1873	David Leo Lawrence	1959–1963
John Frederick Hartranft	1873–1879	William W. Scranton	1963–1967
Henry Martyn Hoyt	1879–1883	Raymond P. Shafer	1967–1971
Robert Emory Pattison	1883–1887	Milton J. Shapp	1971–1979
James Addams Beaver	1887–1891	Richard L. Thornburgh	1979–1987
Robert Emory Pattison	1891–1895	Robert P. Casey	1987–1995
Daniel Hartman Hastings	1895–1899	Thomas Ridge	1995–2001
William Alexis Stone	1899–1903	Mark Schweiker	2001–

PENNSYLVANIA STATE GOVERNMENT

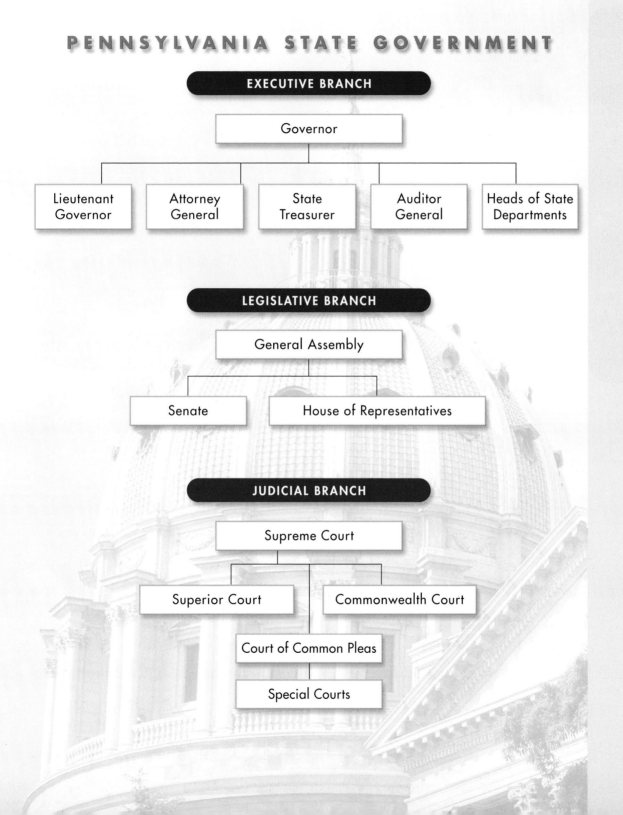

EXECUTIVE BRANCH

Governor

Lieutenant Governor

Attorney General

State Treasurer

Auditor General

Heads of State Departments

LEGISLATIVE BRANCH

General Assembly

Senate

House of Representatives

JUDICIAL BRANCH

Supreme Court

Superior Court

Commonwealth Court

Court of Common Pleas

Special Courts

become a law, it must be passed by a majority in both sections of the General Assembly.

The bill is then sent to the governor. When the governor signs the bill, it becomes a law. If the governor *vetoes*, or refuses to sign a bill, the General Assembly may take another vote and pass the bill without the governor's signature. This is called *overriding* a veto. To override a veto, two of every three members of both parts of the General Assembly must vote in favor of the bill.

JUDICIAL BRANCH

The judicial branch is responsible for determining whether someone has broken a law, and deciding if laws are fair. This is done through the court system. Members of the judicial branch are also responsible for gathering people to serve on a jury, a group of citizens that hears a trial and determines guilt or innocence. Judges make sure that the trial is conducted fairly.

The highest (most important) court in the state is the Pennsylvania Supreme Court. The people elect judges, called justices, for ten-year terms. This court decides if the law in question follows the state constitution. They also make sure that a person tried under a law has been given his or her full rights according to the constitution.

Before a case reaches the supreme court, it is heard in one or more lower-level courts. Pennsylvania has a superior court and a common-

Senators discuss new laws inside the senate chamber of the capitol building.

wealth court. These courts hear appeals in which people are accused of serious crimes called felonies, such as murder or armed robbery.

There are also courts of common pleas, county courts, and probate courts. A probate court rules over the wills and estates of people who have died. A county court rules over county laws, such as traffic violations. The court of common pleas hears lawsuits in which people think they have been treated unfairly and want the court to settle disagreements. For example, a divorce case might be heard in the court of common pleas.

TAXES AND PENNSYLVANIA CITIZENS

The state government provides many services for Pennsylvania residents, such as building roads, parks, recreation facilities, schools, and universities. In order to carry out these programs, the government needs money. To get this money, the state government requires Pennsylvania citizens to pay taxes. Tax money also pays the salaries of the governor and other state officials.

Some taxes are based on income—the money a person earns doing a job. An income tax is a portion of a person's yearly earnings, including pay from work and money earned from investments. Other tax money, called sales tax, comes from goods and services purchased in the state. Taxes on groceries, gasoline, and food served in restaurants are common sales taxes. Businesses also pay tax on the money they make.

TAKE A TOUR OF HARRISBURG, THE CAPITAL CITY

Harrisburg is on the banks of the Susquehanna River. It is small for a state capital, with a population of about 52,000. John Harris founded the city in 1710, when he set up a trading post there. The city is named for Harris's family.

The Capitol Complex is located in the heart of the city. The capitol is modeled after Saint Peter's Cathedral in Rome. When President Theodore Roosevelt attended the opening in 1906, he described the capitol as "the handsomest building I ever saw." It contains more than

The city of Harrisburg is a center for arts and culture, as well as home to more than 50,000 people.

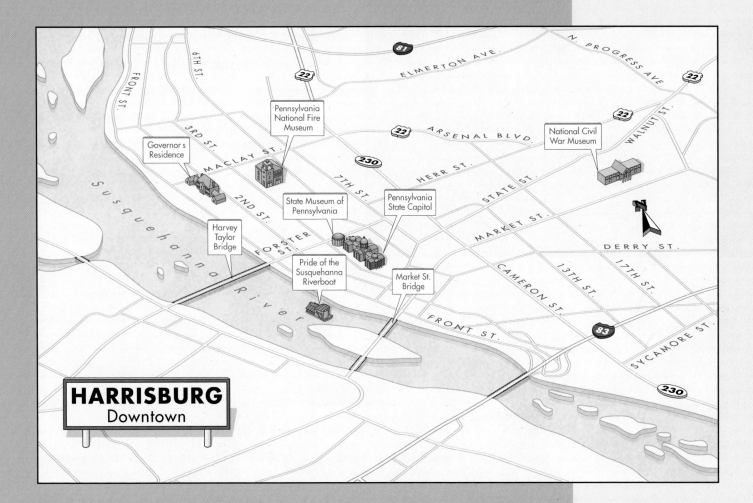

81

22

ELMERTON AVE.

N. PROGRESS AVE.

22

6TH ST.

FRONT ST.

3RD ST.

MACLAY ST.

Pennsylvania
National Fire
Museum

22

ARSENAL BLVD.

WALNUT ST.

22

National Civil
War Museum

Governor's
Residence

2ND ST.

230

7TH ST.

HERR ST.

STATE ST.

State Museum of
Pennsylvania

Pennsylvania
State Capitol

Harvey
Taylor
Bridge

FORSTER ST.

Susquehanna River

Pride of the
Susquehanna
Riverboat

Market St.
Bridge

MARKET ST.

DERRY ST.

CAMERON ST.

FRONT ST.

13TH ST.

17TH ST.

83

SYCAMORE ST.

230

HARRISBURG
Downtown

With its crystal chandeliers and colorful murals, the House of Representatives is breathtaking.

600 rooms. The building has a dome, massive bronze doors, murals, and stained-glass windows. Artist Edwin Austin Abbey painted five murals in the hall of the House of Representatives. Thirty-five of the state's most famous people appear in Abbey's picture, including William Penn and Benjamin Franklin. The capitol welcome center has exhibits showing the state's rich history.

Also in Capitol Park is the State Museum of Pennsylvania, where visitors can investigate Pennsylvania's past. There are exhibits on Earth science, dinosaurs, the military, business, and fine arts. Museum visitors will find a magnificent painting called *The Battle of Gettysburg: Pickett's Charge* on display. It is one of the largest Civil War paintings in the world. A ride on the *Pride of the Susquehanna* offers a full view of the city. This paddlewheeler is historically accurate and a must for city visitors. A tour guide gives a presentation that describes the city and its history during the 45-minute cruise.

The National Civil War Museum opened in Harrisburg in 2001. The museum houses 12,000 Civil War objects. There are personal items from Abraham Lincoln, Jefferson Davis, Ulysses S. Grant, Robert E. Lee, and many other famous people from that era. Displays represent both sides of the war through interactive exhibits, sound and light shows, and video presentations.

CHAPTER FIVE

THE PEOPLE AND PLACES OF PENNSYLVANIA

Pennsylvania has an estimated population of 12,287,150. In the past twenty years, the state's population has decreased by 400,000. The western part of the state, where steel mills and coal mines are found, shows the largest population decrease. This is mostly due to unemployment.

Seven in ten Pennsylvanians live in cities. The state has 16 cities with populations greater than 35,000. These include Philadelphia—the largest city with more than one-and-a-half million people—and Pittsburgh. Other large Pennsylvania cities are Erie, Allentown, Scranton, Reading, and Bethlehem.

Three out of ten Pennsylvanians live in rural, or farm, areas. Major farm areas are located in the southeastern part of the state in Lancaster, Lebanon, York, Berks, and Chester counties. These counties are home to the Pennsylvania Dutch.

Pennsylvania has the third-largest number of Amish people in the United States. Although they live side by side with "the outside world," they keep their own traditions and values.

An Amish barn raising involves the entire community.

THE PENNSYLVANIA DUTCH

The Pennsylvania Dutch were German-speaking people who arrived in Pennsylvania in the 1600s and 1700s. These people spoke *deutsch*, or German, and the English colonists called them "Dutch." Today, Pennsylvania Dutch refers to the region in which these people lived. A number of religious groups settled in the Pennsylvania Dutch region, including the Amish, Mennonites, and Brethren.

Some religious groups in the region live without electricity, cars, and telephones. Rules for using modern technology are set by the local bishop. Health and safety are considered when making such rules. These people are sometimes called Plain Folk because of their "plain" way of living. They dress simply and worship in each other's homes. They travel in horse-drawn carriages and use horses to help with farm work.

Other Pennsylvania Dutch are called the Fancy people. Nine in ten Pennsylvania Dutch wear modern clothing and live like everyone else. They work in cities, drive cars, and use electric washers and dryers.

The plain and fancy Pennsylvania Dutch are linked through their language, art, and food. About 175,000 Pennsylvanians speak a form of Pennsylvania Dutch, although many more people can understand the language. Folk art from this cultural group features many symbols: hearts, tulips, birds, and fancy lettering, called *fractur*. These colorful

Pancake lovers beware! This delicious treat takes pancake eating to a new level. This recipe makes one family-sized pancake, but you may want to double the recipe. This pancake may be gone before you get to the table! Don't forget to ask an adult for help.

PENNSYLVANIA DUTCH APPLE PANCAKE

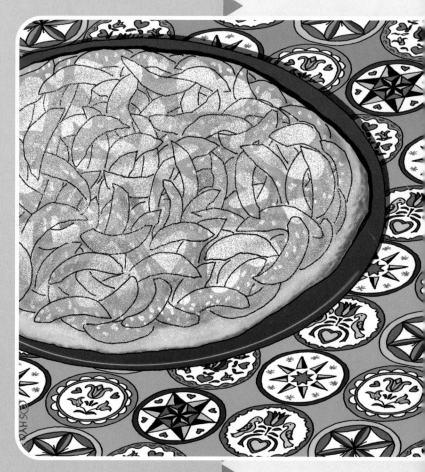

2–3 tablespoons butter or margarine
3 cooking apples, peeled, cored, and cut into
    1/4-inch wedges
2 tablespoons brown sugar
1/2 teaspoon cinnamon
1 egg
1/2 cup milk
1/2 cup Bisquick® or other baking mix
2 tablespoons granulated sugar
powdered sugar

1. Coat apples with brown sugar and cinnamon.
2. Melt butter in frying pan over medium heat. Cook apples in melted butter until just soft, about 5 minutes.
3. While apples are browning, make pancake batter from the egg, milk, baking mix, and granulated sugar.
4. Spread apple mixture evenly over pan. Pour in pancake batter and cover.
5. Cook 4–6 minutes, until pancake is cooked through.
6. Turn pancake out onto large plate. Sprinkle with powdered sugar and serve.

Pennsylvania Dutch folk art designs such as this one are often referred to as "hex signs."

designs, known as hex signs, appear on plates, lampshades, quilts, and other household items, as well as on marriage and birth certificates. Among the foods common to the Pennsylvania Dutch are chicken and dumplings, chicken potpie, schnitzel (veal), spaetzle (homemade noodles), and fastnachts (doughnuts).

EDUCATION IN PENNSYLVANIA

During colonial times, churches provided schools and education. Among the first schools in Pennsylvania was the William Penn Charter School, founded by Quakers in 1689. By the 1800s, the state government began providing education for all children.

Today, children ages eight through sixteen are required to attend school. The statewide public school system is run by a Board of Education that determines what children will learn in class. While most Pennsylvania students attend public school, one interesting exception is the Amish. Amish children learn in one-room schoolhouses built by Amish community leaders. When a school becomes overcrowded, the community elders simply build another one.

Pennsylvania has more than one hundred colleges and universities. Begun in 1740, the University of Pennsylvania claims Benjamin Franklin as one of its founding fathers. The state also supports the Pennsylvania State University system with twenty-three campuses.

MEET THE PEOPLE

When Pennsylvania became an industrial state, Europeans flocked to the mills, factories, and mines. The majority of immigrants were from Germany, Italy, and Ireland. Today, more than three million Pennsylvanians are descended from German relatives. Irish and Italian heritage accounts for another two million people.

In all, almost nine in every ten Pennsylvanians are of European descent, one in ten is African-American, three in one hundred are Hispanic, and two in one hundred are Asian American. Most minorities live in the southeastern corner of the state, with a small group in the Pittsburgh area.

The Native American population in Pennsylvania is quite small, only 18,348 people. Most Pennsylvania Native Americans live in or near Philadelphia and belong to the Susquehanna or Delaware tribes.

WORKING IN PENNSYLVANIA

Pennsylvania has a mixed economy, with a blend of agriculture, manufacturing, and tourism. The national trend in agriculture is for farms to be larger in size but fewer in number. This is also true in Pennsylvania. Today, there are about 50,000 farms in the state, a drop from 155,000 in 1955. Pennsylvania farms provide a wide variety of products. Among these are milk, eggs, nursery plants, corn, tomatoes, pears, and cherries. Grain crops include wheat, hay, oats, barley, and buckwheat. Much of this grain is used for feeding livestock. Livestock operations include beef cattle, poultry, hogs, and sheep.

Dairy farming is one of the most profitable industries in Pennsylvania, which is the nation's fourth-largest milk producer.

Livestock and livestock products are the biggest sellers. Seven in ten farm dollars earned are for milk, cheese, and meat products. Pennsylvania is also the nation's largest producer of mushrooms. Mushrooms are grown in the southeastern corner of the state, where they thrive in warm, damp, dark mushroom houses.

Manufacturing in Pennsylvania has undergone many changes. The major industrial areas in the state are Philadelphia and Pittsburgh. Food processing is the primary manufacturing industry. Hershey, Pennsylvania, is the nation's number one chocolate producer. Pittsburgh is home to the H. J. Heinz Corporation, makers of pickles, soups, sauces, and of course—ketchup. About two in every ten workers are part of the manufacturing industry.

Other manufactured goods include chemicals, electrical equipment, printing, machinery, clothing, and petroleum products. Steel and coal, although less important than they were in the early 1900s, are still vital to the state's economic health.

WHO'S WHO IN PENNSYLVANIA?

Henry J. Heinz (1844–1919) began his profitable vegetable business when he was barely eight years old, selling homegrown horseradish. In 1876, he and his family started the H. J. Heinz Company, known for its pickles, mustard, and ketchup. Heinz was from Pittsburgh.

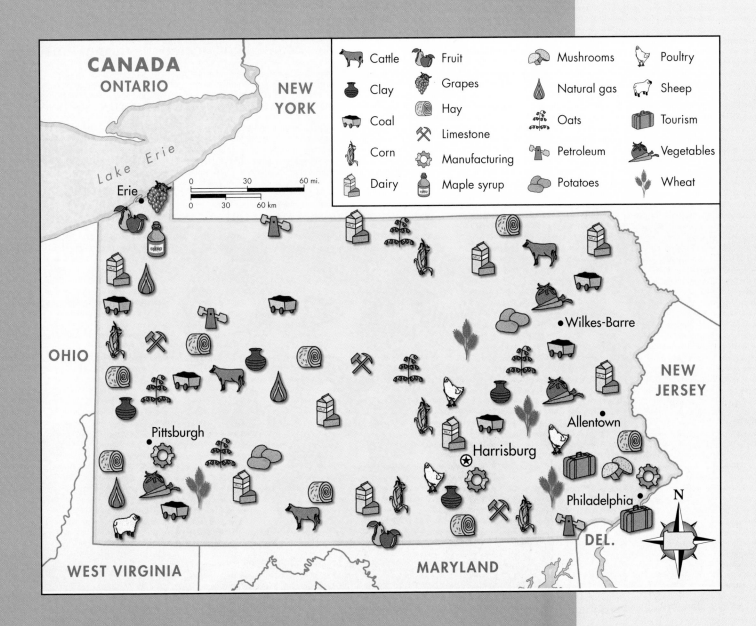

CANADA
ONTARIO

NEW YORK

Lake Erie

Erie

OHIO

NEW JERSEY

Pittsburgh

Wilkes-Barre

Harrisburg

Allentown

Philadelphia

DEL.

WEST VIRGINIA

MARYLAND

N

0   30   60 mi.
0   30   60 km

Cattle
Clay
Coal
Corn
Dairy

Fruit
Grapes
Hay
Limestone
Manufacturing
Maple syrup

Mushrooms
Natural gas
Oats
Petroleum
Potatoes

Poultry
Sheep
Tourism
Vegetables
Wheat

The state takes advantage of its many natural resources. Wells are still drilled for oil and natural gas in the western part of the state. Iron ore is mined throughout the state, as is coal. Major operations quarry limestone and mica, and dig clay.

Four in every ten Pennsylvanians work in service industries, such as health care, teaching, and hotel and restaurant work. Tourism is also part of the service industry and employs many Pennsylvanians. Tourism accounts for all the goods and services provided to people visiting the state, including food, hotel rooms, park and recreation fees, and souvenirs. Roughly 118 million people visited Pennsylvania in 2000. The state offers magnificent scenery in the Pocono Mountains and along the Delaware Water Gap. Philadelphia draws tourists to the Liberty Bell and Independence Hall. The Amish country also attracts many tourists who admire the plain people's traditional ways. In all, tourism brings $20.9 billion into the state.

Many Pennsylvanians, such as these costumed actors at Independence Hall, work in the tourist industry.

Pennsylvania enjoys a rich history in the arts, music, and sports. Since colonial days, the state has attracted people from different races and religions. Each group adds to the varied culture of the state.

Pennsylvania's great artists include portrait painter Benjamin West. He grew up in Springfield and moved to England in 1763, where he painted outstanding portraits of famous people. West was one of the first American artists to gain a reputation in Europe, where he became a favorite of King George III. Another Pennsylvania artist also earned fame in Europe—impressionist Mary Cassatt. Cassatt studied at the Pennsylvania Academy of Fine Arts before moving to Paris in 1866. Among her best-known works is *The Bath,* featuring a mother bathing her child. Pittsburgh's Andy Warhol founded the pop art movement, in which art topics came from popular culture. Warhol once painted a large Campbell's® tomato soup can.

Pennsylvania also claims many great writers. Louisa May Alcott, author of *Little Women,* came from Germantown. More recent novelists include Pittsburgh's Mary Roberts Rinehart and James Michener. Rinehart wrote popular mystery novels, and Michener produced dozens of historical novels. His first successful book was *Tales of the South Pacific;* however, Michener's novels were almost all best sellers.

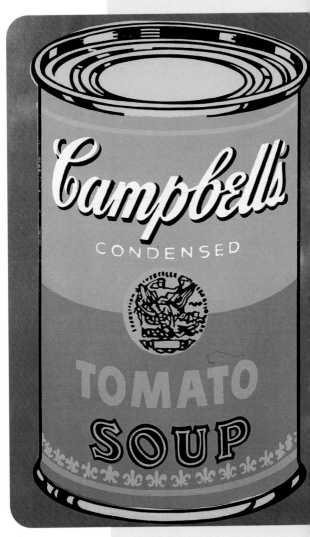

Andy Warhol's painting of a Campbell's soup can is one of his best-known works.

Baseball fans root for the Phillies, a major league baseball team from Philadelphia.

Pennsylvanians also made their mark in movies and television. Singer-dancer Gene Kelly, actress Grace Kelly, and actor James Stewart all came from Pennsylvania. More recently, native Philadelphian Bill Cosby has made millions of people laugh through his heartwarming television shows.

The state boasts a number of professional sports teams. Philadelphia sports fans root for the Phillies during baseball season, the Eagles during football season, the Flyers in hockey, and the Seventy-sixers in basketball. The Pittsburgh Steelers football team won several Super Bowls. The Pittsburgh Pirates baseball team won five World Series. In hockey, five-time NHL scoring champion Mario Lemieux led the Pittsburgh Penguins to two Stanley Cup victories.

TAKE A TOUR OF PENNSYLVANIA

Southeastern Pennsylvania

A tour of Pennsylvania should begin in Philadelphia, the first real city in the state and the birthplace of our country. Start with the Liberty Bell and nearby Independence Hall. There you can see where the Declaration of Independence was signed.

The Liberty Bell may be the most famous cracked bell in the world. When it was first rung in 1752, the bell cracked. Originally, the bell celebrated the fiftieth anniversary of William Penn's Charter of Privileges that guaranteed Pennsylvania citizens the freedom of government. Once cracked, local smiths tried to repair the bell. It rang again on July 8, 1776 to announce the colonists' declaration of freedom from Great Britain. The bell, now cracked beyond repair, rang for the last time in 1846 on Washington's birthday.

For those who enjoy science more than history, try a visit to the Academy of Natural Sciences. This site features an outstanding exhibit about dinosaurs, including skeletons and dinosaur eggs. There are also shows with live animals and videos about plants, animals, and natural events, such as volcanoes and earthquakes.

Students gather round to get a good look at the historic Liberty Bell.

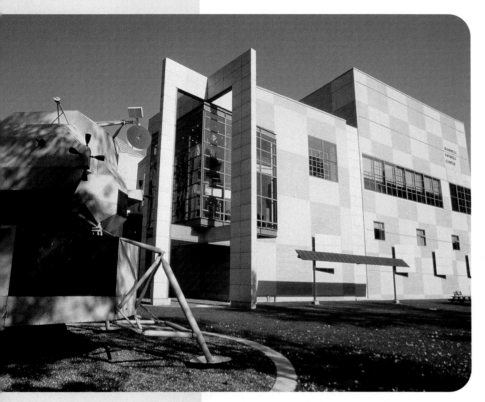

The Franklin Institute is one of the nation's most visited museums.

A great place for children is the Please Touch Museum, where children are told "Hands on" instead of "Hands off." Museum exhibits cover art, science, and history. The museum focuses on exploring the five senses. Expect to hold, smell, see, and listen to a variety of events.

Another science-oriented place is the Franklin Institute. This science museum features exhibits about geography, stars, oceans, mathematics, and weather. Dedicated to Benjamin Franklin, it displays many of his personal belongings. There is also a planetarium with computer-generated videos, a computer show in the Mandell Center, and a theater with an 80-foot- (24-m-) wide screen.

For a slightly different outing, try the Independence Seaport Museum. Among the permanent exhibits are the USS *Becuna* (a 1943 submarine), USS *Olympia* (Admiral Dewey's flagship during the Spanish-American War), and Homeport Philadelphia. These exhibits offer hands-on learning experiences using replicas of cranes to load and unload vessels, along with videos. There is also a Workshop on the Water, where shipbuilders create a variety of small vessels before the watchful eyes of fascinated visitors.

An hour or two outside of Philadelphia is the heart of Pennsylvania Dutch country. Watch out for slow-moving vehicles! Many of the local residents in Lancaster, Strasburg, Bird-in-Hand, and Paradise travel by horse and carriage. Stop in at the arts and crafts stores to see beautiful handcrafted quilts, tinwork lampshades, and classic Amish furniture at the People's Place in Intercourse. Or dine at a Pennsylvania Dutch restaurant and load up on chicken and dumplings.

Hershey is a great destination for chocolate lovers. Learn how cocoa and chocolate are made in the Hershey Chocolate Factory. You'll notice that the streetlights in Hershey have a familiar shape of Hershey's Kisses®. You can't get lost in Hershey—just follow the delicious aroma of chocolate!

With its Kiss-shaped streetlights and the scent of chocolate, Hershey is the perfect place for chocolate lovers.

WHO'S WHO IN PENNSYLVANIA?

Milton Snavely Hershey (1857–1945) began his career in the candy business by working as an apprentice for a Lancaster candy maker. By age eighteen, he had opened his first candy store in Philadelphia. Hershey opened his chocolate factory in 1905 near Derry Church, his birthplace. After the factory opened, the town was renamed Hershey in his honor.

CANADA
ONTARIO

Lake Erie

NEW YORK

National forest, recreation area, or military park
Highway
Capital city
City
Tourist site

0   30   60 mi.
0   30   60 km

Bradford

Titusville

ALLEGHENY
NATIONAL
FOREST

79

Williamsport

Scranton

Germantown

84

80

80

Wilkes-Barre

380

Lehigh

OHIO

New Castle

Oakland

76

Punxsatawney

220

State
College

81

81

80

Bushkill
Falls

DELAWARE
WATER GAP
NAT'L REC.
AREA

NEW
JERSEY

476

79

Pittsburgh

Altoona

99

Johnstown

Hershey

Harrisburg

Carlisle

Easton

Allentown

Bethlehem

476

Washington

70

76

70

76

79

Uniontown

81

GETTYSBURG
NATIONAL
MILITARY PARK

70

Gettysburg

78

Intercourse

Bird in
Hand

Lancaster

York

Strasburg

Paradise

76

Reading

Valley Forge
National
Hist. Park

King of
Prussia

Philadelphia

DEL.

N

WEST VIRGINIA

MARYLAND

66

Northeastern Pennsylvania

A trip to the Pocono Mountains is ideal for hikers, hunters, skiers, and snowboarders. The scenery is magnificent, especially around Bushkill Falls, one of eight waterfalls in the area. The town of Bushkill has Native American exhibits, as well as wildlife exhibits.

Summer and fall draw plenty of tourists to the Delaware Water Gap Recreational Area. Water sports and beaches keep some tourists content in the hot summer sun. Others prefer hiking the area's many nature trails. In autumn, the riverbanks come alive with the golds, reds, yellows, and oranges of fall.

Museum-going visitors to northeastern Pennsylvania will want to visit the Houdini Museum in Scranton. There, tourists learn all about famous magician Harry Houdini and how he performed his amazing escape tricks. The museum shows film clips of Houdini in action—a rare treat for magic lovers.

South of Scranton, Easton offers a unique experience—a tour through the Crayola Factory and Museum. The tour features a three-dimensional sculpture that allows hands-on coloring by visitors. Budding artists can also model their own sculptures in the Crayola computer studio.

South Central Pennsylvania

Near the Maryland border, Gettysburg National Military Park is a must-see, particularly for those interested in the Civil War. It was on this site that more than 43,000 Union and Confederate soldiers lost

Gettysburg National Park stages reenactments of the battle of Gettysburg, the famous three-day battle that was a major turning point in the Civil War.

their lives. It was also where Lincoln gave his famed Gettysburg Address in 1863. Battlefield tours on horseback provide a "cavalry" view of the battlefield.

Western Pennsylvania

In Pittsburgh, animal lovers will enjoy visiting the Pittsburgh Zoo and the Carnegie Museum of Natural History. The zoo features more than 4,000 animals. At the Kid's Kingdom children's zoo, you'll enjoy face-to-face encounters with kangaroos, deer, and goats. There is also a tropical forest complete with gorillas. Don't forget to visit the African grasslands where zebras, elephants, and giraffes roam free.

The Carnegie Museum of Natural History is one of several museums and cultural centers built by Andrew Carnegie. The Museum of Natural History has ten full dinosaur skeletons on display. There are also exhibits about Egypt, the Arctic, and a Discovery Room with hands-on activities for curious learners.

Other features of the Carnegie include a public library, the Andy Warhol Museum, a museum of art, and the Carnegie Science Center. The Science Center is a full-day event with a planetarium, an Omnimax theater, a Science Pier for children, and an aquarium.

Pennsylvania is hunting and fishing, hiking and horseback riding. It is historic battlefields, such as Valley Forge National Park and the Fort Necessity National Battlefield. It is Amish quilts and candles and Hershey's candy. Pennsylvania is the natural beauty of the Allegheny Forest, a wilderness retreat that is spectacular when fall colors are at their height. And it is the modern skyscrapers of Pittsburgh and Philadelphia. No matter what you choose to do, there is plenty of fun to be had in Pennsylvania.

This polar bear finds a welcome home at the Pittsburgh Zoo.

PENNSYLVANIA ALMANAC

Statehood date and number: December 12, 1787, 2nd state

State seal: The Great Seal of Pennsylvania was adopted in 1791. It features a ship, a plow, and bundles of wheat that represent three of the state's counties. An American bald eagle and olive branches symbolize peace.

State flag: The current flag was adopted in 1907. It features the coat of arms from the state seal with two black horses on either side. The state motto is shown on a ribbon underneath the seal. The background is dark blue.

Geographic center: 2.5 miles (4 km) southwest of Bellefonte

Total area/rank: 46,058 square miles (119,290 sq km)/33rd

Borders: New Jersey, Delaware, Maryland, West Virginia, Ohio, New York, and Lake Erie

Latitude and longitude: Pennsylvania is located approximately between 39° 43' and 42° N and 74° 43' and 80° 31' W.

Highest/lowest elevation: Mount Davis, 3,213 feet (979 m) above sea level/sea level, along the Delaware River in southeast Pennsylvania

Hottest/coldest temperature: 111° F (44° C) at Phoenixville, on July 10, 1936/–42° F (–41° C) at Smethport, on January 5, 1904

Land area/rank: 44,820 square miles (116,083 sq km)/32nd

Water area/rank: 1,239 square miles (3,209 sq km)/28th

Population/rank: 12,281,054 (2000 Census)/6th

Population of major cities:
  Philadelphia: 1,517,550
  Pittsburgh: 334,563
  Allentown: 106,632
  Erie: 103,717
  Reading: 81,207

Origin of state name: Means "Penn's woods"; honors William Penn's father. *Sylvania* is from a Latin word meaning "woods."

State capital: Harrisburg (since 1812)

Previous capitals: Philadelphia and Lancaster

Counties: 67

State government: 50 senators, 203 representatives

Major rivers/lakes: Delaware, Monongahela, Allegheny, Schuylkill, and Susquehanna rivers/Raystown Lake, Conneaut Lake, Pymatuning Reservoir

Farm products: Milk, eggs, greenhouse or nursery, corn, hay, barley, tomatoes, pears, cherries, peaches, apples, mushrooms

Livestock: Milk cows, beef cattle, sheep, hogs

Manufactured products: Food processing, electrical equipment, chemicals, machinery, fabricated metals (including steel), chocolate, pharmaceuticals (drugs), medical equipment, clothing, furniture, petroleum refining

Mining products: Coal, natural gas, oil, limestone, clay, mica

Animal: White-tailed deer

Beautification plant: Penngift crownvetch

Beverage: Milk

Bird: Ruffed grouse

Dog: Great Dane

Fish: Brook trout

Flagship: United States Brig *Niagara*

Flower: Mountain laurel

Fossil: *Phacops rana,* a small water animal

Insect: Firefly

Motto: "Virtue, Liberty, and Independence"

Nickname: Keystone State

Song: "Pennsylvania" by Eddie Khoury and Ronnie Bonner

Tree: Hemlock

Wildlife: White-tailed deer, black bears, squirrels, moles, beavers, raccoons, bobwhites, bobolinks, orioles, woodcocks, ruffed grouse, robins, blackbirds

TIMELINE

PENNSYLVANIA STATE HISTORY

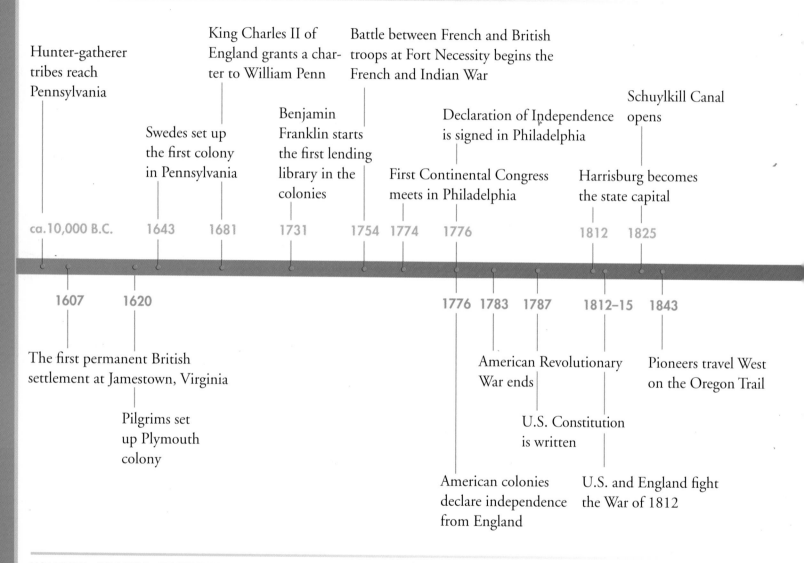

Hunter-gatherer tribes reach Pennsylvania

Swedes set up the first colony in Pennsylvania

King Charles II of England grants a charter to William Penn

Benjamin Franklin starts the first lending library in the colonies

Battle between French and British troops at Fort Necessity begins the French and Indian War

First Continental Congress meets in Philadelphia

Declaration of Independence is signed in Philadelphia

Schuylkill Canal opens

Harrisburg becomes the state capital

ca.10,000 B.C.   1643   1681   1731   1754   1774   1776   1812   1825

1607   1620   1776   1783   1787   1812–15   1843

The first permanent British settlement at Jamestown, Virginia

Pilgrims set up Plymouth colony

American Revolutionary War ends

U.S. Constitution is written

American colonies declare independence from England

U.S. and England fight the War of 1812

Pioneers travel West on the Oregon Trail

UNITED STATES HISTORY

Battle of Gettysburg is fought;
Union army defeats Confederate
troops

Major oil spill on the
Monongahela and Ohio
Rivers near Pittsburgh

First commercial radio
station, KDKA, broad-
casts from Pittsburgh

Governor Tom
Ridge leaves
office to
become the
first Director
of Homeland
Security

Edwin Drake successfully
drills for oil in Titusville

Serious accident
occurs at Three
Mile Island nuclear
power plant near
Harrisburg

Johnstown flood claims more
than 2,000 lives

1859	1863	1889		1920					1979	1988	2001

1846–48	1861–65		1917–18	1929	1941–45	1950–53	1964	1965–73	1969		1991	1995

U.S. takes part in
World War I

Civil rights laws
passed in the U.S.

U.S. and other nations
fight in Persian Gulf War

U.S. fights in
World War II

U.S. fights
war with
Mexico

U.S. fights in the
Vietnam War

The stock market
crashes and U.S.
enters the Great
Depression

U.S. fights in the
Korean War

Civil War
occurs in the
United States

U.S. space shuttle
docks with Russian
space station

Neil Armstrong
and Edwin
Aldrin land on
the moon

GALLERY OF FAMOUS PENNSYLVANIANS

Louisa May Alcott
(1832–1888)
Author of *Little Women* and *Little Men*. Alcott also served as a nurse during the Civil War. Born in Germantown.

Marian Anderson
(1897–1993)
First African-American to perform at New York City's Metropolitan Opera House. Born in Philadelphia.

James Buchanan
(1791–1868)
Former congressman, senator, and the fifteenth United States president. During Buchanan's administration, Oregon and Minnesota became states, and the Pony Express brought mail service to the West. Born in Cove Gap.

Rachel Carson
(1907–1964)
A marine biologist (a scientist who studies sea mammals) and the author of *Silent Spring* and *The Sea Around Us*. Carson began the environmental movement by revealing the dangers of chemicals such as DDT. Born in Springdale.

Bill Cosby
(1937–)
A comedian, television star, and generous contributor to education and the arts. The first African-American to star in a network television show. Born in Philadelphia.

David O. Selznick
(1902–1965)
Producer of well-known films, such as *Gone with the Wind* and *King Kong*. Born in Pittsburgh.

Ida M. Tarbell
(1857–1944)
Popular journalist and editor. Known for her articles on illegal practices in politics and business, particularly against Standard Oil Company. Tarbell was the most famous female journalist of her time. Born in Erie County.

Andrew Wyeth
(1917–)
An artist famous for his realistic art style. Born in Chadds Ford.

GLOSSARY

amendment: a change in a law or document

cabinet: group of advisors of a governor or president

capital: the city that is the center of a state or country government

capitol: the building in which a government meets

census: an official counting of a country's population

climate: the weather conditions of a particular area

constitution: document that sets out the basic rules and laws of a government and lists the rights of people ruled by that government

distill: a process to make something pure, or free of contamination

economy: the way people produce and use goods; how people make money

executive branch: group that runs a state or government

extinction: when no more members of an animal species are living

governor: an elected person who leads the state

immigrant: person who leaves one country to move into another country

inauguration: ceremony in which a government official is sworn into office

judicial: judges and courts

legislature: a group of people who make laws

manufacture: to make products by hand or machinery

militia: everyday citizens who learn how to fight in the event of an emergency

mural: a painting applied directly to a wall

neutral: not taking either side in a disagreement

plateau: a raised land region

population: the number of people living in a region

prosperity: a period of wealth or success

strike: refusing to work until certain demands or conditions are met

strikebreakers: workers brought in to replace people on strike

tourism: businesses that provide hotels, restaurants, and entertainment for visitors

transportation: a system of roads, trains, buses, and airports

unemployment: the condition of being unable to find a job

union: an organized group of workers who unite for a specific purpose

FOR MORE INFORMATION

Web sites

Official Pennsylvania Home Page

http://www.state.pa.us
Links to information about Pennsylvania's government and tourist attractions.

Pittsburgh City Site

http://www.city.pittsburgh.pa.us
Includes information about events and sights in Pittsburgh.

Philadelphia City Site

http://www.phila.gov
Information for visitors, residents, and businesses in Philadelphia.

Amish Community Site

http://www.800padutch.com/amish.html
Questions and answers about the "Plain People" of the Pennsylvania Dutch Country.

Books

Cole, Michael D. *Three Mile Island: Nuclear Disaster.* Berkeley Heights, NJ: Enslow, 2002.

Giblin, James, and Michael Dooling. *The Amazing Life of Benjamin Franklin.* New York, NY: Scholastic, 2000.

Gross, Virginia T. *The Day It Rained Forever: A Story of the Johnstown Flood.* New York, NY: Puffin, 1993.

Knight, James E. *Seventh and Walnut: Life in Colonial Philadelphia.* Mahwah, NJ: Troll, 1999.

Lutz, Norma Jean, and Arthur M. Schlesinger, Jr. *William Penn: Founder of Democracy.* Broomall, PA: Chelsea House, 2000.

Addresses

Bureau of Travel Marketing
Pennsylvania Department of Commerce
453 Forum Building
Harrisburg, PA 17120

Pennsylvania Government
Office of the Chief Clerk
Pennsylvania House of Representatives
House Post Office
Main Capitol Building
Harrisburg, PA 17120

Chamber of Business and Industry
417 Walnut Street
Harrisburg, PA 17120

Office of Philadelphia City Representative
1600 Arch Street, 13th floor
Philadelphia, PA 19103

INDEX

ABOUT THE AUTHOR

Barbara Somervill's first visit to Pennsylvania was a family trip to the Pennsylvania Dutch country. She still remembers the delicious chicken and dumplings and apple pancakes she had on the trip. To find information for this book she checked a number of sources: the Internet, chambers of commerce and tourist bureaus, and the local library.

Barbara was raised and educated in New York. She's also lived in Toronto, Canada; Canberra, Australia; California; and South Carolina. She is the mother of four boys, two dogs, and a cat, and the proud grandmother of Lilly.